Beyoncé I

By United Library

https://campsite.bio/unitedlibrary

Table of Contents

Disclaimer

This biography book is a work of nonfiction based on the public life of a famous person. The author has used publicly available information to create this work. While the author has thoroughly researched the subject and attempted to depict it accurately, it is not meant to be an exhaustive study of the subject. The views expressed in this book are those of the author alone and do not necessarily reflect those of any organization associated with the subject. This book should not be taken as an endorsement, legal advice, or any other form of professional advice. This book was written for entertainment purposes only.

Introduction

Beyoncé delves into the life and career of one of the most iconic figures in modern music and pop culture. Beyoncé Giselle Knowles-Carter, affectionately known as "Queen Bey," has captivated audiences worldwide with her unparalleled vocal prowess, electrifying performances, and unapologetic artistry. This book takes you on a journey through the remarkable trajectory of a woman who has not only redefined the music industry but has also left an indelible mark on society.

From her early beginnings as a young, talented performer in singing and dancing competitions to her rise to stardom as a member of the record-breaking girl group Destiny's Child, Beyoncé's journey is one of resilience and dedication. With her debut solo album, "Dangerously in Love," she soared to solo stardom, setting the stage for a series of chart-topping albums that would solidify her status as a global superstar.

But "Queen Bey" didn't stop at music. She evolved into a multifaceted businesswoman, creating her own management company, Parkwood Entertainment, and exploring societal themes through groundbreaking visual albums like "Beyoncé" and "Lemonade."

In this meticulously researched biography, we explore her record-breaking achievements, her chart-topping hits, and her groundbreaking visual storytelling. With an impressive 32 Grammy Awards and countless other accolades to her name, Beyoncé's influence on the music industry and popular culture is immeasurable.

This book is a celebration of an artist who has shattered boundaries, empowered women, and become an inspiration to millions around the world. Join us as we journey through the life and legacy of the woman who has truly defined the 21st century.

Beyoncé Knowles

Beyoncé, sometimes called by her full name Beyoncé Knowles, sometimes by her married name Beyoncé Carter, born September 4, 1981 in Houston, Texas, is an American singer, songwriter, dancer, music producer and actress.

In 2009, she was named artist of the decade 2000 by *The Guardian*, while *New Musical Express* saw her as one of the artists who defined the decade 2010. In 2013, *New Yorker* music critics described Beyoncé as the most popular, important and influential musician of the early 21st^e century. In 2013, *Forbes* magazine ranked her 17e in the list of most powerful women and 4e in the list of most powerful stars in the world, making her the second most powerful singer in the world, behind Lady Gaga and ahead of Madonna. In 2014, she topped *Forbes* magazine's list of the world's most influential celebrities. In 2022, *Rolling Stone* magazine declared her the greatest musical artist of the past decade.

In January 2017, she had sold over 185.5 million records worldwide, to which can be added the 65.5 million copies sold with the group Destiny's Child, of which she was the frontwoman.

Beyoncé has won numerous awards over the course of her career, making her the second most awarded artist in the world after Michael Jackson. At the Grammy Awards, she is the most awarded artist with 32 awards. In 2022, Beyoncé totaled 88 nominations, making her the most nominated artist in Grammy Awards history, tied with her husband Jay-Z. In 2007, she made history by becoming the first female artist to win the International Artist Award at the American Music Awards. She is ranked as the fourth artist of the 2000s by *Billboard*, and on December 11, 2009, *Billboard* magazine ranks her as the most successful female artist and the most played artist on radio in the decade 2000-2009. Her 2016 hit *Formation* becomes the most awarded song in history, surpassing Michael Jackson's hit *Thriller.*

On January 21, 2013, she sings the national anthem at the second inauguration of U.S. President Barack Obama. In February 2013, she sang at the half-time show of Super Bowl XLVII. She sang again at Superbowl 50 in February 2016, accompanied by Coldplay and Bruno Mars. Both shows are among the most viewed half-time shows of all time.

Beyoncé Knowles also has an acting career: she first appeared on screen in 2001 in the musical film *Carmen: A Hip Hopera*, followed by *Dreamgirls* in 2006, for which she received two Golden Globe nominations. She also played one of the lead roles in the 2009 thriller *Obsessed.*

Beyoncé and her mother Tina launched their family fashion line, *House of Deréon*, in 2004. She also advertises for brands such as Pepsi, Tommy Hilfiger, Giorgio Armani and L'Oréal.

Beyoncé is the mother of three children born to her husband, rapper and businessman Jay-Z.

Biography

Youth and beginnings

Beyoncé Giselle Knowles was born on September 4, 1981 in Houston, Texas. She is the daughter of Mathew Knowles, a professional music producer, and Celestine Ann "Tina" Beyoncé, a stylist, dressmaker and hairdresser of Louisiana Creole origin. On her mother's side, Beyoncé is a descendant of Acadian chief Joseph Brossard' . Another of her ancestors is Albert de Cuir, originally from Macon, in the province of Hainaut, who moved to Louisiana in 1720 and became a slave owner. Beyoncé is named after her mother, whose maiden name is "Beyoncé". Her younger sister Solange Knowles will also be a singer.

Beyoncé attends St. Mary's Elementary School in Texas, where she takes dance lessons. Her talent for singing was discovered when her dance teacher began humming a song she finished, reaching high notes. Beyoncé's interest in music and performing began after she took part in a school talent show, singing John Lennon's *Imagine* and winning the contest' . At the age of seven, Beyoncé began to attract press attention, being mentioned in the *Houston Chronicle* as a candidate for *The Sammy* local performing arts awards.

In the fall of 1990, she enrolled at Parker Elementary School, a music school in Houston, where she practiced on stage with the school choir. She also attended Kinder High School for the Performing and Visual Arts in Houston, and later entered Alief Elsik High School in the Houston suburb of Alief . Beyoncé is a soloist in the choir of her church, St. John United Methodist Church. She remained in the choir for two years.

At the age of nine, Beyoncé met LaTavia Roberson at an audition to join an all-girl entertainment group. Along with LaTavia and her cousin Kelly Rowland, the three of them join a six-girl rap and dance group originally called *Girl's Tyme*. West Coast RnB producer Arne Frager travels to Houston to meet them, and, convinced, takes them to record at his The Plant Recording Studios in Northern California, featuring the voice of Beyoncé. As part of the effort to sign Girl's Tyme to a major label, Frager's initial strategy is to get them on *Star Search*, the biggest talent search show of the day. Girl's Tyme entered the competition, but failed because, according to Beyoncé, the song they performed was the wrong . Beyoncé suffered her first "professional failure" with this defeat, but regained her confidence after learning that pop stars Britney Spears and Justin Timberlake had also experienced the same humiliation.

To manage the band, Beyoncé's father, a medical equipment salesman at the time, resigned from his job in 1995, setting up a "boot camp" for their training. This cut Beyoncé's family budget in half, and her parents were forced to move into separate apartments. Shortly after Rowland's inclusion, Matthew reduces the group to four, with LeToya Luckett joining them in 1993. Rehearsing in Tina's hairdressing salon and backroom, the small group continues to perform, as if opening for an all-girl RnB band of that era; Tina contributes by designing their costumes, which she will continue to do throughout the Destiny's Child era. Thanks to Matthew's continued support, they audition for record labels and finally sign with Elektra Records. They move to Atlanta to work on their first recording, before the label breaks the contract in 1995. The group returned home to start afresh, and the name was changed to Destiny's Child. This brought discord to the Knowles family, and Beyoncé's parents separated briefly when she was 14. In 1996, the family reformed, and at the same time, the girls signed a contract with Columbia Records under the name Destiny's Child.

Destiny's Child (1997-2001)

The group changed its name to Destiny's Child in 1993, after a passage from the Book of Isaiah. Together, they performed at local concerts and, after four years on the road, the group signed to Columbia Records at the end of 1997. That same year, Destiny's Child recorded their first song, *Killing Time*, for the soundtrack of the 1997 film *Men in Black'* . The following year, the group released their debut album, which contained their first hit, *No, No, No*. This album established the group in the music industry, with moderate sales and earning the group three Soul Train Lady of Soul Awards for "Best RnB/soul single" with *No, No, No*, "Best RnB/soul album of the year" and "Best new RnB/soul or rap artist". The band released their second multi-platinum album, *The Writing's on the Wall*, in 1999. The album features some of the band's best-known songs, such as *Bills, Bills, Bills*, the group's first number-one single, *Jumpin', Jumpin'*, and *Say My Name*, which would become their most successful song at the time, and would remain one of their signature songs. *Say My Name* won Best RnB Performance by a Duo or Group with Vocals and Best RnB Song at the 43ᵉ Grammy Awards ceremony in 2001. *The Writing's on the Wall* has sold over eight million copies.

Luckett and Roberson discover in the video for *Say My Name* that they have been replaced by Michelle Williams and Farrah Franklin. They sue the band for breach of contract. Eventually, Luckett and Roberson left the band. Franklin followed them five months later, as evidenced by her absence from promotions and concerts. She attributes her departure to negative vibes in the band resulting from the split. After deciding on their final numbers, the trio record *Independent Women Part I*, which appears in 2000 on the soundtrack to the film *Charlie's Angels*. It became their highest charting single, remaining at the top of the Official US Singles Chart for eleven consecutive weeks. Later that year, Luckett and Roberson withdraw their complaint against the new former band members, while continuing their lawsuit against Mathew. Both parties agree to cease their public denigration. Luckett and Roberson file suit again after the release of Destiny's Child's third album, *Survivor*, in May 2001, claiming that the songs on the album were aimed at them. The album debuted at number one on the U.S. *Billboard* 200, selling 663,000 copies. Two years later, *Survivor* has sold over ten million copies worldwide, over 40% of them in the U.S. alone. The album spawned other number-one singles such as *Bootylicious* and the album's eponymous track, *Survivor*; the latter would earn the group a Grammy Award for Best R&B Performance by a Duo or Group with Vocals. After the release of their Christmas album, *8 Days of Christmas*, the group announces a break for each of them to pursue solo projects.

Dangerously In Love and disbandment of the band (2000-2005)

Before embarking on her solo career, when she was still with Destiny's Child, Beyoncé was already making solo appearances. She duetted with label mate Marc Nelson on the song *After All Is Said and Done for the* soundtrack of the 1999 film *The Best Man*. In early 2001, while Destiny's Child finished recording *Survivor*, Beyoncé landed a starring role in the MTV TV movie *Carmen: A Hip Hopera*, alongside American actor Mekhi Phifer. Shot in Philadelphia, the film is a modern interpretation of the 19th[e] century opera *Carmen by* French composer Georges Bizet.

In 2002, Beyoncé co-stars in the *Austin Powers* comedy *Goldmember*, playing Foxxy Cleopatra alongside Mike Myers, and records her first solo single, *Work It Out*, for the film's soundtrack. The following year, she starred alongside Cuba Gooding Jr. in the romantic comedy *The Fighting Temptations*, and recorded numerous songs for the film's soundtrack, including *Fighting Temptation* and a cover of *Fever* .

That same year, Beyoncé appeared on her boyfriend Jay-Z's single *03 Bonnie & Clyde*. She also records a version of 50 Cent's *In da Club*, released in March 2003. Luther Vandross and Beyoncé cover the duet *The Closer I Get to You*, originally recorded by Roberta Flack and Donny Hathaway in 1977. Their version won a Grammy Award for Best R&B Performance by a Duo or Group with Vocals the following year, while *Dance with My Father*, a Vandross cover, rewarded Beyoncé with the Grammy Award for Best Male R&B Vocal Performance'.

After Williams and Rowland released their respective solo albums, Beyoncé in turn released her first solo album, *Dangerously in Love*, in June 2003. Featuring a number of musical collaborators, the album contains a combination of songs with high rhythms and RnB melodies. The album debuts at #1 on the *Billboard* 200, selling 317,000 copies in its first week. Certified quadruple platinum on August 5, 2004 by the Recording Industry Association of America, the album has sold 6.7 million copies to date in the United States. The album produced two number-one singles. *Crazy in Love*, featuring a rapped verse by Jay-Z, was released as the album's first single, and remained at number one on the *Billboard* Hot 100 for eight consecutive weeks, and on numerous charts worldwide. Beyoncé also topped the UK singles and album charts simultaneously'. The album's second single, *Baby Boy,* featuring dancehall singer Sean Paul, also became one of the biggest hits of 2003, dominating the US radio airplay chart and staying at number one on the *Billboard* Hot 100 for nine weeks, one week longer than *Crazy in Love'*. Like Crazy in Love, the next three singles also became commercial successes, propelling the album to the top of the charts and keeping it there, eventually being certified multi-platinum. Beyoncé wins a then-record five Grammy

Awards at the 48ᵉ Grammy Awards ceremony in 2004 for her solo work, which includes the Grammy Award for Best Female R&B Vocal Performance for *Dangerously in Love 2*, Best RnB Song for *Crazy in Love*, and Best Contemporary 'B' Album. She shares this record with four other female artists: Lauryn Hill in 1999, Alicia Keys in 2002, Norah Jones in 2003 and Amy Winehouse in 2008. She broke her own record in 2010, with 6 Grammy Awards in a single ceremony. In 2004, she won a Brit Award for International Female Solo Artist. In early 2004, Beyoncé sang the American national anthem at Super Bowl XXXVIII at Houston's Reliant Stadium. On February 27, 2005, she took part in the 77ᵉ Oscars ceremony, performing *Vois sur ton chemin*, the song from Christophe Barratier's film *Les Choristes,* nominated for the Oscar for Best Film Score.

She then plans to release a sequel to *Dangerously in Love*, using some of her leftover recordings. However, her musical aspirations have been put on hold due to a busy schedule, including recording with Destiny's Child on what will be their final album. After three years devoted to solo projects, Beyoncé, Rowland and Williams released *Destiny Fulfilled* in November 2004. The album peaked at number two on the *Billboard* 200, and spawned three top-40 singles, including *Lose My Breath* and *Soldier*. To accompany the album, Destiny's Child launched the *Destiny Fulfilled... And Lovin' It* world tour in 2005, which ran from April to September. During their visit to

Barcelona, the band announced that they would be disbanding after the North American leg of the tour' . In October 2005, the group released a compilation, called *Number 1's*, featuring all Destiny's Child's number-one singles and most of their well-known songs. The compilation also includes three new songs. Destiny's Child was honored with a star on the Hollywood Walk of Fame in March 2006. They were also recognized as the world's best-selling female group of all time by the World Music Awards' .

B'Day and Dreamgirls (2006-2007)

Continuing her film career, Beyoncé plays the role of Xania, an international pop star in the film *The Pink Panther*, alongside Steve Martin, who plays Inspector Jacques Clouseau' . The film was released on February 10, 2006, and debuted at number one at the box office, grossing $21.7 million in its first week. Beyoncé recorded *Check on It for the* film's soundtrack, with Slim Thug, and reached number one on the *Billboard* Hot 100. In late 2005, she again put her second album on hold after landing a role in *Dreamgirls*, a film adaptation of the 1981 Broadway musical of the same name about a 1960s band loosely based on the all-female Motown group The Supremes. In the film, she plays a Diana Ross-inspired character, Deena Jones' . *Dreamgirls, starring* Jamie Foxx, Eddie Murphy and Jennifer Hudson, was released in

December 2006. Beyoncé recorded several songs for the film's soundtrack, including *Listen*. On December 14, 2006, Beyoncé was nominated for two Golden Globes thanks to the film: the Golden Globe for Best Actress in a Motion Picture Musical or Comedy and the Golden Globe for Best Original Song for *Listen*. Inspired by her role in *Dreamgirls*, Beyoncé works on her second album without a clear plan, telling MTV News, "[When filming ended] I had so much pent-up, so many emotions, so many ideas. Beyoncé surrounds herself with her former musical collaborators, including Rich Harrison, Rodney Jerkins and Sean Garrett, at Sony Music Studios in New York. She co-wrote and co-produced almost all the songs on the album, which was recorded in three weeks. *B'Day* was released worldwide on September 4, 2006, and the following day in the U.S. to coincide with the celebration of her twenty-fifth birthday. The album debuts at #1 on the *Billboard* 200, selling over 541,000 copies in its first week, its highest first-week sales ever as a solo artist. The album was certified three times platinum in the U.S. by the Recording Industry Association of America (RIAA). The first single, *Déjà Vu*, a duet with Jay-Z, reached number one in the UK. *Irreplaceable* is released in October 2006 as the album's second single worldwide and third single in the United States. The song tops the *Billboard* Hot 100 for 10 consecutive weeks, Beyoncé's record. Although it was a commercial success, the album's relatively short production run was criticized' .

Beyoncé re-releases *B'Day* on April 3, 2007, in a deluxe edition featuring five new songs and the Spanish versions of *Irreplaceable* and *Listen. At the same time,* the *B'Day Anthology* is released with 10 video clips' . In parallel with the album, Beyoncé embarks on the long concert tour *The Beyoncé Experience*, which visits over ninety venues worldwide, and is filmed for the concert DVD *The Beyoncé Experience Live!* At the 49e Grammy Awards in 2007, *B'Day* wins Beyoncé the award for Best Contemporary RnB Album. The artist made history at the 35e annual American Music Awards by becoming the first woman to win the International Artist Award.

I Am... Sasha Fierce and *Cadillac Records* (2008-2010)

Beyoncé releases her third studio album, *I Am... Sasha Fierce*, on November 18, 2008. She declares that *Sasha Fierce is the* name of the personality she adopts when she's on stage. The album is preceded by the release of her two singles, *If I Were a Boy* and *Single Ladies (Put a Ring on It)*. While *If I Were a Boy* topped many charts around the world, especially in European countries, *Single Ladies (Put a Ring on It)* reached number one on the *Billboard* Hot 100 for four non-consecutive weeks, giving Beyoncé her fifth number-one single in the United States.

Beyoncé plays the role of blues singer Etta James in the musical biopic, *Cadillac Records*. Her performance in the film earns her critical acclaim. The song *Once in a Lifetime, a* collaboration with British singer Scott McFarnon, is nominated for a Grammy Award and a Golden Globe. Beyoncé also stars with Ali Larter and Idris Elba in a thriller called *Obsessed*, which had been in production since May 2008. The film proved to be a commercial success, opening in the U.S. on April 24, 2009 and grossing $11.1 million on its opening day. It ended the opening weekend in first place, with a total of $28.6 million.

Halo, the fourth single from *I Am... Sasha Fierce* takes the fifth position on the *Billboard* Hot 100, becoming Beyoncé's 12e top ten single on this chart as a solo artist. This makes Beyoncé the female artist with the most top ten hits on the Hot 100 this decade' . She is also the female artist with the most cumulative weeks at number one on this chart this decade, with a total of 36 weeks at number one, the most top fives and also the most top tens of the decade with fourteen' , as well as the most singles in the top 40 during the decade with 19 singles.

Beyoncé wins Best Female Artist at the 2009 NAACP Image Awards. She also wins Best RnB Artist at the 2009 Teen Choice Awards. On January 18, 2009, Beyoncé was at the Lincoln Memorial festivities in honor of the inauguration of Barack Obama, the 44e President of the United States. She also sang her version of Etta James' most famous classic RnB song, *At Last*, to President Obama and his wife Michelle, who performed their first dance as President and First Lady on January 20, 2009, at the Neighborhood Inaugural Ball.

In support of the album, Beyoncé launched the extensive I Am... World Tour in the summer of 2009, touring the globe. She concludes the North American leg of her tour with a limited four-day engagement at the intimate 1,500-seat Encore Theatre at Steve Wynn's *Encore* Resort in Las Vegas, from July 30 to August 2, 2009. As of August 2, 2009, Beyoncé's tour is officially ranked the number one attraction, thanks to record attendance and a brand-new, multi-stop itinerary.

The music video for *Single Ladies (Put a Ring on It)* wins the 2009 BET Awards for Video of the Year. In addition, it is nominated for a total of nine awards at the 2009 MTV Video Music Awards, ultimately winning Video of the Year and two other awards, although its failure in the Best Female Video category, won by Taylor Swift and her song *You Belong with Me,* leads to controversy at the ceremony" . In October 2009, Beyoncé received Billboard magazine's "Woman of the Year" award. In November 2009, she was announced as the winner of 4Music's

"World's Greatest Pop Stars" competition. Over 100,000 people voted.

Following the 2010 earthquake in Haiti, Beyoncé took part in the *Hope for Haiti Now: A Global Benefit for Earthquake Relief*. She appears in London with Jay-Z, Rihanna, Bono and U2's The Edge, where she performs an acoustic version of her song *Halo*. Beyoncé dominates the 52e Grammy Awards ceremony, receiving 10 nominations, including the Grammy Award for Album of the Year for *I Am... Sasha Fierce*, Recording of the Year for *Halo*, and Song of the Year for *Single Ladies (Put a Ring on It)*. Her other two nominations are the Grammy Award for Best Traditional R&B Vocal Performance for *At Last* and Best Song Written for Film, Television or Other Visual Media for *Once in a Lifetime* from *Cadillac Records* in 2009. Along with Lauryn Hill, she thus achieves the most Grammy Award nominations for a single ceremony by a female artist. She finally set the record for the most Grammy Awards won at a single ceremony by a female artist on January 31, 2010, when she won six of her ten nominations. She wins Song of the Year, Best RnB Song and Best Female RnB Vocal Performance for *Single Ladies (Put a Ring on It)*, Best Female Pop Vocal Performance for *Halo*, Best Contemporary RnB Album for *I Am... Sasha Fierce* and the Grammy Award for Best Traditional RnB Vocal Performance for *At Last*.

The last two weeks of the *I Am... World Tour take place in* February 2010 in South America and the Caribbean. In March 2010, Lady Gaga's single *Telephone*, featuring Beyoncé, reaches number one in the Pop Songs chart, becoming the sixth number one in the chart for both singers. With this performance, they equal Mariah Carey's record for most number ones since the launch of the Nielsen BDS chart based on radio airplay in 1992. *Telephone* becomes Beyoncé's fifth number-one song in the UK Singles Chart, as a solo artist, as a lead artist or not.

Earlier in the year, Beyoncé declared in an interview with *USA Today* that she would be taking a musical break in 2010: "It's definitely time to take a break, recharge my batteries. I'd like to take about six months and not go into the studio. I just need to live my life, be inspired by new things." Beyoncé also says she wants to go out to eat, take classes, see movies, Broadway shows and also plans to spend more time with her nephew, Julez (the son of her sister, Solange Knowles)'''' .

During her hiatus, Beyoncé was interviewed by *Allure* magazine in February 2010, where she revealed that "Sasha Fierce is no more. I killed her." She goes on to say that she's comfortable enough with herself to go without an alias. She further explains, "I don't need Sasha Fierce anymore, because I've grown up and now I'm able to unify the two." At the 2010 BET Awards, Beyoncé wins the BET Award for Video of the Year for her collaboration with Lady Gaga on *Video Phone*.

4 (2011-2012)

In January 2011, it was announced that Beyoncé would star in a remake of *A Star is Born*, directed and produced by Clint Eastwood for Warner Bros. The remake will be the fourth adaptation of the story of *A Star is Born*, and the most recent since the 1976 version starring Barbra Streisand and Kris Kristofferson. However, on October 9, 2012, Beyoncé tells *E! News* that she has dropped out of her planned role in the film due to scheduling issues. She says: "For months, we've been trying to coordinate our schedules to bring this remake into view, but it's just not possible. Hopefully, in the future, we'll have a chance to work together. In February 2011, documents obtained by the website WikiLeaks revealed that Beyoncé along with Usher, Mariah Carey and Nelly Furtado had been paid no less than $1 million to sing in front of family members of the then Libyan leader Muammar Gaddafi. *Rolling Stone* magazine reported that the music industry urged them to return the money they earned for the concert. On March 2, 2011, a spokesperson for the singer told *The Huffington Post* that she had donated the money to the Clinton Bush Haiti Fund, which was set up to help victims of the 2010 earthquake in Haiti. On March 28, 2011, it was announced that Beyoncé's father and long-time manager Matthew Knowles was no longer managing her career. The singer's publicist sends a statement to Associated Press, saying that she and her father have parted ways "professionally". She now manages herself and has hired her own management team. In June 2011, *Forbes placed* her eighth on its list of "Highest-Paid Celebrities Under 30" for earning $35 million between May 2010 and May 2011. The magazine explains that Beyoncé's low ranking is due to the fact that she spent most of this period on the road and was in the process of recording her fourth album.

Beyoncé's fourth studio album, *4*, was released on June 24, 2011. The album is inspired by artists including Fela Kuti, The Stylistics, Lauryn Hill, Stevie Wonder and Michael Jackson. It debuts at #1 on the *Billboard* 200, selling 310,000 copies in its first week. This gives the singer her fourth consecutive #1 album in the U.S., and she becomes the second female artist, and third artist, to have her first four studio albums at #1 on the *Billboard* 200. However, the first-week sales of *4* are Beyoncé's lowest first-week sales with a studio album to date. Her first single *Run the World (Girls)* peaks at 29e on the *Billboard* Hot 100, becoming the singer's first lowest charting single as a solo artist. The second single from the album *Best Thing I Never Had is* released on June 1er 2011. It reached 16e on the *Billboard* Hot 100. She also performed at the T in the Park Festival in Scotland on July 9, 2011 and the Oxegen Festival in Ireland the following day. Beyoncé takes to the stage at New York's Roseland Ballroom for four nights of special concerts. The concert program for *4 Intimate Nights with Beyoncé* is the entire *4* album. Over four evenings, August 14, 16, 18 and 19, she performs her new songs to a standing-room-only audience.

On August 28, at the 2011 MTV Video Music Awards, Beyoncé announced that she and Jay-Z were expecting their first child. She made the announcement during her red carpet appearance and at the end of her performance of *Love on Top*, rubbing her belly' . *The Huffington Post* later confirmed that the singer was 5 months pregnant and that this pregnancy announcement broke the record for "most tweets recorded per second for a single event" on Twitter with 8,868 tweets per second. MTV reports that Beyoncé's performance on *Love on Top* and her pregnancy announcement at the awards ceremony helped the 2011 MTV Video Music Awards become the most viewed program in MTV history with 12.4 million viewers. What's more, Google Insights data shows that the most searched term from August 29 to September 4, 2011 was "pregnant Beyoncé", which reached "bursting" levels - a term Google uses to describe a search with an increase of over 5,000%. Beyoncé's announcement of her pregnancy led to an increase in sales of her albums, particularly *4*, which had sold 700,000 copies by August 2011. The album was certified platinum by the RIAA. *4* has sold 1,400,000 copies in the U.S. and over 3 million copies worldwide.

On October 8, a pre-recorded performance of Beyoncé performing Michael Jackson's *I Wanna Be Where You Are* is broadcast at the Michael Forever tribute concert at the Millennium Stadium in Cardiff, Wales. In November 2011, Beyoncé Knowles is named the world's highest-earning performer per minute by the social media website, earning £1.25 million for a five-song concert at a 2010 New Year's Eve party on the island of St. Barthélemy, equivalent to £71,040 per minute spent on stage. On November 30, 2011, she received two nominations for the 54e Grammy Awards: one for Best Rap/Vocals Collaboration for *Party* and one for Best Long Form Music Video for the *I Am... World Tour*. In December 2011, the singer placed fourth on *Forbes* magazine's 2011 list of "Highest-Paid Women in Music" for earning $35 million. On December 20, 2011, it is revealed that Knowles has been working with producer The-Dream to record new songs. In an interview with *The Boombox*, The-Dream explains, "She's ready to work ... She's crazy! She never stops doing anything. I don't know if [pregnancy] will slow her down. She's just amazing at doing things, I don't know how she's going to do it, she's just crazy ... in a good way."

The Mrs. Carter World Tour and *Beyoncé* (2013-2015)

On January 21, 2013, Beyoncé sings the national anthem at the second inauguration of U.S. President Barack Obama. On January 29, 2013, Destiny's Child release a compilation entitled *Love Songs* with an unreleased song *Nuclear*, their first original song since their split in 2005. On February 3, 2013, she sings at the Super Bowl XLVII halftime show, which has become one of the most viewed halftimes of all time with 104 million viewers and is the second most commented event on Twitter. A few days later, at the 55th Grammy Awards, she wins Best Traditional RnB Song for *Love on Top*.

She appears in her own documentary she directs and produces entitled *Life Is But a Deam* broadcast on HBO on February 16, 2013 where she talks about her professional and personal life including her pregnancy' . The DVD, accompanied by a live performance as part of *Revel Presents: Beyoncé Live* was released in November 2013 with an exclusive song; *God Made You Beautiful*.

Beyoncé kicks off her 132-date fifth *The Mrs. Carter Show World* Tour on April 15, 2013, in Belgrade, Serbia, ending on March 27, 2014, in Lisbon, Portugal. Her tour is one of the most profitable tours of all time.

On April 4, 2013, she appeared in an *Embrace your past, but live for now* advert for beverage brand Pepsi-Cola, where part of the unreleased track Grown Woman was played. The following day, a new song *Standing on the Sun* is broadcast in an advert for clothing brand H&M. In May 2013, she takes part in the Jay-Z-produced soundtrack to *Gatsby the Magnificent,* covering Amy Winehouse's *Back to Black* in collaboration with André 3000. She lends her voice to Queen Tara in the animated film *Epic: The Battle of the Secret Kingdom,* released on May 24, 2013, and records the track *Rise-Up* co-written with Sia for the film. In July 2013, she appears on the Jay-Z album, *Magna Carta... Holy Grail* with the track *Part II (On the Run),* which was released as the third single from the album in February 2013.

On December 13, 2013, Beyoncé released her fifth self-titled album *BEYONCÉ* including 14 songs and 17 videos, with no ads or promotion, which topped the *Billboard* 200 for three consecutive weeks and she became the first female artist with five consecutive albums to reach number one on the chart. After 3 days of sales on iTunes, it managed to reach number 1 in 104 countries, and the total number of albums sold in three days is 828,773, which becomes the absolute world record in such a short period. The album sold 420,000 copies in 24 hours in the U.S. alone, and the surprise release generated 1.2 million tweets in 12 hours. In five days, it sold a million copies on iTunes. As of November 2014, the album has sold over 5 million copies worldwide.

The first two singles from the album were released a few days after the album's release, *XO peaked at* number forty-five on the *Billboard* Hot 100, while *Drunk in Love* in collaboration with Jay-Z was a huge commercial success, reaching number two on the chart, and the couple performed the song as the opening performance at the 56th Grammy Awards. On February 25, 2014, *Partition* is released, reaching number twenty-three on the chart, followed by *Pretty Hurts* on June 10, 2014, which, like *Partition*, tops the Hot Dance Club Songs chart. A reissue of the album is released on November 24, 2014; from which three singles are taken: a remix of *Flawless* in collaboration with Nicki Minaj on August 12, 2014, then *7/11* on November 24, 2014 which reached number thirteen on the Billboard Hot 100 and topped the Hot Dance Club Songs as well as the Hot R&B/Hip-Hop Songs, as well as *Ring Off* which is released a few days later. On June 2, 2014, her collaboration with Kelly Rowland and Michelle Williams, *Say Yes* is released, which appears on the latter's *Journey to Freedom* album released in September 2014.

In April 2014, after several weeks of rumors, Beyoncé and Jay-Z announced their twenty-one-date joint tour entitled *On The Run Tour*, which kicked off in the U.S. on June 25, 2014 and ended at the Stade de France on September 12 and 13, 2014. At the 57th Grammy Awards, she is nominated in six categories, of which she wins three; Best

RnB Performance and Best RnB Song for *Drunk in Love*
and Best Surround Sound Album for her self-titled album,
she does not, however, win Album of the Year, to
everyone's surprise' .

Lemonade and *Everything is Love* (2016-2018)

On February 6, 2016, she released the single *Formation*,
the video for which was released exclusively on Tidal,
reaching number ten on the *Billboard* Hot 100. The
following day, she sang the song at the Superbowl, where
she performed the half-time show with Coldplay and
Bruno Mars. Following this performance she announced
her seventh world tour, *Formation World Tour,* which
kicked off on April 27, 2016.

On April 23, 2016, she created an event with the surprise
release of her sixth studio album, *Lemonade.* She had
announced on April 16, 2016 that a 60-minute
documentary called *Lemonade* would be broadcast on
HBO without saying the nature of the project, although
fans and the media quickly came to deduce that it would
be an album. The same day that the opus is released on
Tidal, it is officially released worldwide the following day.
It debuted at #1 on the *Billboard* 200, selling 653,000
copies in its first week of release. She breaks DMX's
record as the only artist to have her first six albums top
the chart, and also beats Taylor Swift as the first artist to
have twelve songs from the same album chart in the

Billboard Hot 100 (Taylor's was eleven). The album is critically acclaimed and is her best-received project by any critic. On May 3, 2016, she released the second single, *Sorry*, which reached number eleven on the *Billboard* Hot 100, then followed by the third single *Hold Up*, which reached number thirteen on the same chart. Many media and fans report that this album is an undertone to her husband Jay-Z's infidelity, despite their multiple collaborations. At the MTV Video Music Awards in August 2016, she won eight of her eleven nominations, the most important of which was Video of the Year for *Formation*, making her the most awarded artist in the ceremony's history. In January 2017, her Instagram pregnancy announcement became the site's most liked photo in less than a few hours.

At the 59^e Grammy Awards ceremony in February 2017, she was the most nominated artist with nine nominations, making her the most nominated female artist in the history of the ceremony. She won only two awards: Best Video for *Formation* and Best Urban Album for *Lemonade*. Surprisingly, she did not win Album of the Year for *Lemonade, which was the* subject of controversy in the media and on social networks" . The award was won by Adele, who declared during her speech that *Lemonade* deserved the prize and broke it to give the other part to Beyoncé' . In September 2017 Beyoncé released the remix of *Mi Gente* in collaboration with J

Balvin and Willy William. All proceeds from this music were donated to charities helping victims of hurricanes Harvey and Irma, which hit Texas, Mexico, Puerto Rico and other Caribbean islands. *Mi Gente* is considered by *Billboard* to be one of the 100 songs that defined the 2010s, having reached number three on the Hot 100.

On November 10, 2017, Eminem unveiled *Walk on Water*, the lead single from his *Revival* album, in collaboration with Beyoncé.

On November 30, Ed Sheeran announced that Beyoncé would sing in the remix of his music *Perfect*, which was released on December 1, 2017 as *Perfect Duet*. The song becomes number 1 on the Billboard charts. It is the sixth song in Beyoncé's solo career to accomplish this.

On January 4, 2018, the music video for Beyoncé and Jay-Z's collaboration on the latter's new album, *4: 44*, *Family Feud* is released. It is directed by Ava DuVernay.

On March 1, 2018, DJ Khaled unveils *Top Off* in collaboration with Beyoncé, Jay-Z and Future. This is the first single from DJ Khaled's *Father of Asahd* album" .

On March 5, 2018, the announcement of a joint tour between Beyoncé and Jay-Z leaked on Facebook. But it wasn't until March 12 that the couple officially announced their world tour, *On the Run II Tour* through a trailer on Youtube.

On March 20, 2018, Beyoncé and Jay-Z left for Jamaica to shoot a music video directed by Melina Matsoukas' .

On April 14 and 21, 2018, Beyoncé takes part in the Coachella Festival in California and delivers two performances considered by critics to be committed and historic for the African-American community. She becomes the first black woman to headline the California festival. 125,000 people saw Beyoncé surrounded by a live orchestra, over 100 dancers and her Destiny's Child friends, who joined her for part of the show. The festival marks Beyoncé's comeback after being pregnant with her twins'' .

On June 6, 2018, Beyoncé and her husband Jay-Z kick off the *On the Run II Tour* in Cardiff, UK. Ten days later, during their final performance in London, the duo unveil *Everything is Love*, their joint album credited as The Carters ("Les Carter" in French). The couple also post a music video for the album's lead single, *Apeshit,* on Beyoncé's Youtube channel, shot at the Louvre Museum' . *Everything is Love* received mostly positive reviews' , and debuted at number two in the U.S. charts with 123,000 album equivalents (for 70,000 physical albums sold).

On December 2, 2018, Beyoncé and Jay-Z headline the *Global Citizen: Mandela 100* festival at FNB Stadium in Johannesburg, South Africa. Their two-hour performance adopts a similar structure to their On the Run II Tour, and

Beyoncé is praised for outfits that pay tribute to African diversity' .

On March 30, 2019, against Chadwick Boseman, LeBron James, Regina King and Ryan Coogler, she won the special *Entertainer of the Year* award at the 50th NAACP Image Awards ceremony.

Homecoming, The Lion King, Black is King (2019-2021)

On April 17, 2019, *Homecoming*, a concert-documentary retracing Beyoncé's historic performance at the 2018 Coachella festival, will be released on Netflix. The film's release is accompanied by the surprise release of a live album *Homecoming: The Live Album*. It was later revealed that Beyoncé and Netflix had signed a $60 million deal to produce three different projects, including *Homecoming*. *Homecoming* was nominated in 6 categories at the 71st Creative Arts Emmy Awards.

Beyoncé doubles the voice of Nala in the original version of the remake of The *Lion King*, released in cinemas on July 19, 2019' . The singer also participates in the film's soundtrack with, for example, the July 11, 2019 release of a cover of *Can You Feel the Love Tonight* with Donald Glover, Billy Eichner and Seth Rogen, originally composed by Elton John. Beyoncé is also creating original songs for the film, such as "Spirit", released as the lead single from both the film's soundtrack and Beyoncé's new project *The*

Lion King: The Gift. The latter is an album produced and directed by Beyoncé. The singer says she was inspired by R&B, pop, hip hop and Afro Beat. The songs are all produced with African producers to find the "authenticity and heart" (Beyoncé) of this film set in Africa' .

On April 29, 2020, Megan Thee Stallion released the remix of her song *Savage* in collaboration with Beyoncé' . This music - Beyoncé's first of 2020 - climbs to number one on the Billboard Hot 100 and becomes the eleventh Beyoncé song to achieve this success.

On June 19, 2020, in the midst of the Black Lives Matter movement in the United States, Beyoncé released *Black Parade*, a committed song reminding us of the cultural and artistic value of black people in the country. Profits from the song are donated in support of black businesses notably affected by the COVID-19 crisis.

On July 31, 2020, Disney+ is releasing *Black Is King*, a visual album, which is a set of music videos for *The Lion King: The Gift.* The film is produced by Disney and Parkwood Entertainment' . With this latest album, Beyoncé is the most nominated artist at the 63rd Grammy Awards ceremony, walking away with four of them, making her the most awarded female singer, the most awarded female artist and the second most awarded Grammy artist of all time.

September 4, 2021 Beyoncé announces in *Harper's Bazaar* magazine on September 4, 2021 that she is preparing her new album.

On November 12, 2021, Beyoncé releases *Be Alive*, a song she wrote and recorded for the biographical film about *The Williams Method*, and which is shortlisted for the Oscars' . On March 27, 2022, Beyoncé gave her first live performance in two years, singing the song at the 94th Academy Awards.

2022: *Renaissance*

On June 10, 2022, Beyoncé fans and some media outlets noticed updates on her website and social networks that could herald an imminent album release' . These speculations were confirmed on June 16, 2022 with the announcement by streaming platform Tidal, and then by the singer herself on her website and networks, of a new album, *Renaissance*, scheduled for July 29, 2022. British Vogue devotes its July cover to the American star, suggesting that the album will be a tribute to house sounds in particular. The album's lead single, *Break My Soul*, inspired by 1990s house music, was released on June 21, 2022" and became the most played song on American radio of the year.

On July 1er 2022, Beyoncé unveils the cover of her new album.

The album *Renaissance* was released on July 29, 2022, and is available for listening on online platforms. In the week of its release, *Renaissance* became the most listened-to album in France, a first for Beyoncé, and in the United States.

Under fire from controversy, Beyoncé's team has announced that they are re-recording part of the song *Heated* to replace the term *spaz*, deemed offensive to people with disabilities.

On August 12, 2022, Beyoncé released the official teaser visuals for her album .

In January 2023, she announced a world tour with two dates in France, in Paris and Marseille (May and June 2023).

Musical style and image

Music and voice

Beyoncé has always been identified as the centerpiece of Destiny's Child. Jon Pareles of the *New York Times* believes that she defines the group, calling her voice "velvety but tangy, with an insistent tremolo and reserves of breathtaking soul". Other critics praise her vocal range and power. Reviewing her second album *B'Day*, *Entertainment Weekly*'s Jody Rosen writes: "Beyoncé Knowles is a storm in singer's clothing. On her second solo album, *B'Day*, the songs come in huge bursts of rhythm and emotion, with Beyoncé's voice undulating over clattering rhythms; you have to look far - perhaps in the halls of the Metropolitan Opera - to find a singer who sings with such pure force... No one - not even R. Kelly, nor Usher, to say nothing of her pop diva rivals - can match Beyoncé's genius for gliding her voice over a hip-hop beat".

Chris Richards of the *Washington Post* writes, "Even when she's coasting, she soars above her imitators. It's all in her voice, a superhuman instrument capable of punctuating any beat with goosebump-inducing whispers or enormous diva roars. Distressed, scorned, in love or hostile, Beyoncé pulls it all off with undeniable virtuosity."

Cove magazine ranks Beyoncé seventh on its "100 Best Pop Singers" list, giving her 48 out of a possible 50 points based on several criteria ranging from her vocal ability to her harmony. Beyoncé has often been criticized for singing with too many ornaments. This has earned her frequent comparisons with artists like Mariah Carey, whose vocal embellishments are deemed by some to be "detrimental" to the melody of her songs. *Eye Weekly* writes: "There's no doubt that Beyoncé is one of the best pop singers, perhaps one of the best alive.... [However] however judicious her singing may be, the overall effect still feels like an iron fist in a velvet glove."

Beyoncé's music is generally described as contemporary RnB, but she also incorporates other genres such as pop, funk, hip-hop and soul. Although the singer almost exclusively releases songs in English, Beyoncé did record a few songs in Spanish for the *B'Day* re-release. Destiny's Child had already recorded a Spanish song and received a warm welcome from their Latin fans. Beyoncé learned Spanish at school when she was young, but she doesn't have much of it left. Before recording the Spanish tracks for the *B'Day* reissue, she was coached phonetically by American record producer Rudy Perez.

Composition and production

As soon as she joined Destiny's Child, Beyoncé became artistically involved. She co-wrote most of the songs recorded by the group, as well as her own. Known for her personal songwriting and empowerment of women, she says Jay-Z's presence in her life has changed her thoughts on the relationship between men and women. Some of her songs are autobiographical, or drawn from the experiences of her friends.

Beyoncé also co-produces most of the recordings she is involved in, particularly during her solo period. If she doesn't compose the music herself, she usually contributes melodies and ideas during production. Beyoncé gained recognition as a songwriter during the operation of Destiny's Child in the 1990s and into the mid-2000s. She won the Pop Songwriter of the Year award at the 2001 American Society of Composers, Authors and Publishers Pop Music Awards, becoming the first African-American woman and the second female songwriter of all time to achieve this feat . The same year, Beyoncé composed *Irreplaceable*, *Grillz* (*Soldier* is sampled on the song) and *Check on It*, becoming the only woman to do so since Carole King in 1971 and Mariah Carey in 1991. In terms of credits, she is tied with Diane Warren for third place with nine number-one singles.

Scene

In 2006, Beyoncé introduced her all-female touring band Suga Mama, featuring bassists, drummers, guitarists, horn players, keyboardists and percussionists. The band debuted at the 2006 BET Awards and reappeared in the music videos for *Irreplaceable* and *Green Light*. The band accompanies Beyoncé in her live performances, notably on The Beyoncé Experience world tour in 2007, and the I Am... World Tour in 2009.

In an article entitled *Born to Entertain,* Beyoncé, alongside classical and contemporary artists, receives praise for her stage performances. Jarett Wieselman of the *New York Post* ranks the singer first on his list of the top five singer/dancers and writes "the megastar consistently devotes every ounce of herself to choreography." Reviewing the I Am... World Tour in 2009, Alice Jones of the *Independent* writes, "Watching Beyoncé sing and strut her stuff can at best make us feel intimidated, or, at worst, hallucinate. She takes her role as an artist so seriously that she's almost too beautiful". *The New York Times* writes: "there's a breathtaking elegance in her acute desire to entertain". Renee Michelle Harris of the *South Florida Times* writes that Beyoncé "takes the stage with arrogance and intensity... She showcases her powerful voice without missing a note, while vigorously performing perfectly executed dance moves.... No one, not Britney [Spears], not Ciara [Harris] and not Rihanna can offer what she does, - a complete assortment of voice, movement and presence." The *Daily Mail* writes: "Many industry pundits have elevated Beyoncé to 'the next Michael Jackson'. While it's far too early for such comparisons, she has certainly proved that she is one of the most exciting and talented artists and can thus claim to go down in history as such."

Critics also praise her vocal qualities on stage. Reviewing one of her performances, Jim Farber of *The Daily News* writes: "Beyoncé made her vocal cords sound as hard as steel. When the horn melody fades, she glides over it with athletic ease. The way Beyoncé uses her body intensifies the sense of triumph. With her hair in teased Medusa braids, a perpetual pelvic roll and legs long enough to make Tina Turner proud, Beyoncé's presence punctuates her song with an exclamation point." Stephanie Classen of *StarPhoenix* says: "Beyoncé is no ordinary performer.... From the very first note, the 27-year-old powerhouse rises above all gimmicks, mastering the show like a supremely sexy alien princess. Only extraterrestrial origins could explain this voice... [Beyoncé] could make a fool of any other pop star today." *Newsday* writes: "She proves that sexy choreography and powerful vocals don't have to be mutually exclusive... No playback worries here."

Beyoncé was also criticized for her suggestive choreography. Her performance at the grave of former US President Ulysses S. Grant on July 4, 2003 was for some too lascivious; indeed, Grant's descendants had mixed reactions to it.

Sasha Fierce

Following the release of her third studio album *I Am...
Sasha Fierce*, Beyoncé introduces her alter-ego Sasha
Fierce to the world. Beyoncé says Sasha was born during
the filming of her 2003 hit *Crazy in Love*. In an interview
with *People* magazine, Beyoncé claims that her alter-ego
is strictly for the stage, with the article's writer describing
Sasha Fierce as the singer's sensual, aggressive alter-ego.
She later explains to MTV: "Sasha Fierce is fun, the most
sensual, the most aggressive, the most outspoken side
and the even more glamorous side that comes out when
I'm working and when I'm on stage.". Later interviewed by
Marie Claire, she reveals that she feels possessed by her
alter-ego on stage: "I've created an alter-ego: what I do
when I'm on stage, I would never normally do. I reveal
things about myself that I wouldn't in an interview. I have
out-of-body experiences [on stage]. If I cut my legs, if I
fall, I didn't even feel it. I'm so fearless that I'm not aware
of my face or my body.

Image

She declares, "I like to dress sexy and act like a lady," but
also explains that the way she dresses on stage is "just for
the stage." A fashion fan, Beyoncé combines her artistic
elements with her music videos and shows. According to
Italian fashion designer Roberto Cavalli, she uses different
styles and tries to harmonize them with the music at her
shows. The *B'Day Anthology Video Album* features

numerous fashion-oriented sequences, showcasing a wardrobe ranging from classic to contemporary. *People* magazine recognizes Beyoncé as the best-dressed celebrity of 2007. Beyoncé's mother publishes a book in 2002, *Destiny's Style: Bootylicious Fashion, Beauty and Lifestyle Secrets From Destiny's Child*, which explains how fashion has had an impact on Destiny's Child's success.

Her beauty style, however, is sometimes criticized as an apology for "bleached" beauty. Indeed, the singer has a habit of appearing in public with her hair openly bleached in European shades, or with hair extensions, again in shades and shapes totally unnatural for an African-American woman. The scandal of her transformation in the media was brought to light during the L'Oréal ad episode: she appears with a lightened complexion, straight chestnut hair and eyes that look natural, but have in fact been lightened to brown via digital retouching software (her real eyes being black). The brand later apologized for having altered the photo so much.

As one of the most exposed black female celebrities in the U.S., Beyoncé has often received criticism that some believe to be racism or sexism. Journalist Toure of *Rolling Stone* magazine declared that since the release of *Dangerously in Love*, "[Beyoncé] has become half Halle Berry sex symbol..." In 2007, she was featured on the cover of *Sports Illustrated Swimsuit Issue*, becoming the first woman, neither model nor athlete, to pose for the magazine and the second African-American to do so, after Tyra Banks. The same year, Beyoncé appears on billboards and newspapers across the U.S. showing her with an antique cigarette holder in hand. Used for the back cover of *B'Day,* the image provoked a reaction from an anti-smoking group, indicating that she didn't need to add the cigarette holder "to look more sophisticated".

On April 24, 2009, Beyoncé appeared on *Larry King Live,* where she took on a more political image and talked about everything from her song at President Barack Obama's inauguration to the racism she faced because of her origins. She says Michelle Obama is "very chic", and even said that singing at the Obamas' first dance was the highlight of her career.

Accusations of plagiarism

In October 2011, Beyoncé was accused of plagiarism by Anne Teresa De Keersmaeker in connection with the video *Countdown* , which largely reproduces the choreography, sets and costumes of two films based on works by the Flemish choreographer: *Rosas danst Rosas* (1983) and *Achterland* (1990). In response, the singer issued a statement admitting that she had been inspired by de Keersmaeker's work.

Influences and heritage

Many artists have influenced Beyoncé's musical style. She grew up listening to the songs of Anita Baker and Luther Vandross, with whom she would eventually collaborate, but she often mentions her pop hero, Michael Jackson, and pop icon Madonna as the reasons she makes music. She was also exposed to the jazz of Rachelle Ferrell, having sung her songs during vocal lessons. Beyoncé cites her influences from American artists such as Tina Turner, Aaliyah, Prince, Aretha Franklin, Whitney Houston, Janet Jackson, Selena, Mary J. Blige, Diana Ross, Donna Summer, Mariah Carey and Colombian singer Shakira. She also mentioned that one of her favorite artists is British singer Sade.

Beyoncé also influences many contemporary artists. In addition, *American Idol* season 6 winner Jordin Sparks' debut single *Tattoo*, as well as her debut album, have been described as very similar to Beyoncé's style; some critics have even said that *Tattoo* could be "a blatant rip-off" of Beyoncé's single *Irreplaceable*. Stephen Thomas Erlewine of AllMusic finds the songs of American pop singer Katharine McPhee, on her self-titled debut album, heavily influenced by Beyoncé's music. Kelly Rowland was also inspired by Beyoncé's voice when recording her second album, *Ms. Kelly*. Miley Cyrus tells *Seventeen*

Magazine: "I want to be like Beyoncé. She's the ultimate woman. You look at her and you don't wonder what her private life might be like. You look at her and think: 'That girl on stage is a superstar'. You don't care about anything else; all you care about is her music. So I hope that will be me in the future." Meanwhile, Cheryl Cole tells *Hello Magazine* that she sees in Beyoncé "the aspiration every woman should have." In June 2010, Michael Menachem of *Billboard magazine* praised the song *Impossible* sung by Barbadian Shontelle, comparing the poignancy and technical precision with Beyoncé's song *Irreplaceable*. Beyoncé is the most nominated female artist at the Grammy Awards, with 53 nominations. In 2004, she became one of only five women to win 5 Grammy Awards in a single ceremony, before breaking her own record in 2010 with 6 Grammys in a single evening, a record for a female artist.

Beyoncé becomes the first woman to win the International Artist Award at the American Music Awards. At the 2008 World Music Awards, Beyoncé is honored with a Legend Award for Outstanding Contribution to the Arts. Beyoncé is also the lead singer of one of the world's best-selling female groups: Destiny's Child. Her debut album is included in the Rock and Roll Hall of Fame's final list of the top 200 albums in music history. The singer is one of the few artists of her generation to be mentioned on this list. Many wax statues have been made in

Beyoncé's image, including one in the Madame Tussauds wax museum. Mo'Nique presented the BET Awards 2003, 2004 and 2007, and was apparently inspired by Beyoncé, since she decided to open the 2004 ceremony by performing Beyoncé's song *Crazy in Love*. She repeated the feat in 2007 with *Déjà Vu*. In December 2009, Beyoncé was ranked by Billboard magazine as the most successful female artist of the decade 2000-2010. She also tied with fellow pop star Rihanna for the most number-one singles in the U.S. in the decade 2000-2010. Beyoncé is ranked by the RIAA as the most certified artist of the same decade.

Single Ladies (Put a Ring on It) became very popular, and critics often compared it to Aretha Franklin's *Respect* or Gloria Gaynor's *I Will Survive.* Many people have posted videos of themselves on YouTube trying out the choreography from the music video.

In 2016, singer Beyoncé continues to be a figurehead for the Black Panther Party, making former activists like Ericka Huggins proud. She pays tribute to the BPP at the 50th Super Bowl.

Other activities

House of Deréon

In 2005, Beyoncé and her mother launched House of Deréon, a contemporary ready-to-wear line for women. The concept is inspired by three generations of women in their family, with the name Deréon paying homage to Beyoncé's grandmother, Agnèz Deréon, who worked as a seamstress' . According to Tina Knowles, the overall style of the line best reflects Beyoncé's taste and style. Launched in 2006, House of Deréon products could be seen during the group's shows and tours during the *Destiny Fulfilled* period'' . The stores, which have a presence in the USA and Canada, sell sportswear, fur jackets, clothing and accessories including handbags. Beyoncé has also teamed up with House of Brands, a local shoe company, to produce a range of shoes for House of Deréon. In 2004, Beyoncé and her mother founded their family company, Beyond Productions, to license and manage the House of Deréon brand. In early 2008, they launched Beyoncé Fashion Diva, a mobile game with an online social networking function, with House of Deréon.

Animal rights organization People for the Ethical Treatment of Animals (PETA) has criticized Beyoncé for her use of animal fur in her clothing line. The organization sent letters of protest and invited the celebrity to a dinner on the issue. Beyoncé never responded.

Products and advertising

In 2002, Beyoncé signed a promotional contract with Pepsi-Cola. The contract includes TV, radio and Internet advertising. She is hired by the company to help reach a wider demographic. A 2004 Pepsi TV ad in the theme of "Gladiators" features Beyoncé and singers Enrique Iglesias, Britney Spears and Pink. The following year, she appeared with Jennifer Lopez and David Beckham in a commercial called "Samurai". The range of products with which Beyoncé has commercial agreements also includes beauty products and fragrances, although the singer is allergic to perfume. Beyoncé has worked with L'Oréal since the age of eighteen. She launched Tommy Hilfiger's True Star fragrance in 2004 and sang a cover of *Wishing on a Star* for the True Star ads, for which she received $250,000. She also launched Hilfiger's True Star Gold in 2005 and Emporio Armani's Diamonds in 2007. *Forbes* magazine reports that Beyoncé earned $80 million between June 2007 and June 2008, between her album, tour, fashion business and advertising contracts. This makes her the second-highest paid music personality in the world during this period. In 2009, *Forbes* ranked Knowles fourth on its list of the 100 most powerful and influential celebrities in the world, third on its list of musicians, and number one on its list of highest-paid celebrities under 30, with over $87 million in earnings between 2008 and 2009. The same magazine ranks Beyoncé third on its list of the most powerful celebrities of 2010 with $87 million gross thanks to her 93-date world tour, her contracts with Nintendo and L'Oréal and her House of Deréon clothing line. Beyoncé is also listed at number two on the list of the 100 most powerful and influential celebrities in the world, and subsequently proved to be the highest-paid female artist' .

Knowles launches her first fragrance, Heat, in 2010. As part of the perfume's advertising campaign, Knowles re-released her cover of *Fever* for the Heat ads. Knowles first released Fever for her 2003 film *The Fighting Temptations*. Industry experts estimate that the fragrance could make $100 million in global retail sales in its first year. Beyoncé explains the fragrance concept: "A lot of my concerts involve the use of fire, so we thought of 'Heat'. Also, red is one of my favorite colors, as is gold. Everything, from the bottle design to the name to the ideas for the ads, came from me." Beyoncé also explains about the fragrance: "For me, a fragrance reflects a woman's attitude and personal sense of style; while I love different fragrances, I've never found one that really characterizes me as a woman. Working with Coty, I was able to materialize my ideal fragrance by creating a seductive, sophisticated scent; one that reflects my inner strength." In March 2013, H&M announced Beyoncé as the new face of its 2013 swimwear collection.

Sasha Fierce clothing line

On July 1er 2009, Beyoncé and her stylist mother, Tina, launched a line of *back-to-school* womenswear inspired by the tour costumes for the album. The collection also includes sportswear, outdoor wear, handbags, shoes, eyewear, lingerie and jewelry, with the exception of Sasha Fierce's metal glove and ticket fan. The series of outfits is intended to match the pop star's on-stage persona. The look is streamlined, very form-fitting with lots of metallic accessories, including a black bodysuit and lots of leggings. Beyoncé explains: "The line really brings out another side of my personality, which I'm grateful I can express. The Sasha Fierce line brings out a woman's confidence, sensuality and bold side."

Commitments

For the first twenty years of her career, she refrained from any public political involvement. On the contrary, she paid $2 million for Hannibal Kadhafi, son of Libyan leader Muammar Kadhafi, on New Year's Eve in Saint-Barthélémy in 2010.

She declared herself a feminist in 2013, on the release of her fifth studio album *Beyoncé* . The following year, at the MTV Music Awards, the term *Feminist* was displayed in large letters while she was on stage: according to author Sandrine Galand in her book *Le féminisme pop* (éditions du Remue-ménage), "what Beyoncé did on the evening of August 24, 2014, was to project feminism onto the *mainstream* scene", at a time when feminist discourse was still marginal or confined to well-identified activist circles.

However, Beyoncé's feminist commitment is debated between, on the one hand, an uninhibited, sexualized display of her body, as seen in tracks such as (*Blow*, *Partition)*, and sexy on-stage outfits such as mini-shorts or plunging necklines, and on the other hand, overtly feminist songs such as *Run the World (Girls)* or *Flawless.* In 2014, feminist intellectual bell hooks denounced the artist's hypersexualization and declared that "part of

Beyoncé" appeared to her to be "actually anti-feminist [and even] terrorist, particularly in terms of its impact on young girls"; she later qualified her remarks while retaining reservations about Beyoncé's feminism. Nigerian feminist Chimamanda Ngozi Adichie, whose song *Flawless featured* Beyoncé's speech in favor of girls' rights, disassociated herself from the artist in 2016, declaring that Jay-Z takes up too much space in her life.

She denounced racist police violence in her track *Formation* during the Super Bowl half-time show in February 2016. This commitment continued on the *Lemonade* album released a few weeks later, where she clearly spoke out against police violence in the United States, of which black people are the primary victims, while insisting: "Anyone who perceives my message as anti-police is completely mistaken. I have so much admiration and respect for the police officers and police families who sacrifice themselves for our safety. But let's be clear: I'm against police brutality and injustice. They are two different things. After the deaths of Alton Sterling and Philando Castile in Dallas in July 2016 followed by the murders of white police officers, she took part in the collective video *23 Ways You Could be Killed If You're Black*. Headlining the Coachella festival in 2018, she sang *Lift Every Voice and Sing*, considered the national anthem of African-Americans, and in 2020 her *Black Parade* video echoed the murder of George Floyd and the anti-racist protests that followed. According to academic Keivan Djavadzadeh, she is "one of the most visible figures in pop culture among those committed to Black Lives Matter" and "her activism is not lukewarm: she makes donations and relays the messages of the movement, whose strategy is precisely based on making systemic racism visible".

Like her husband, she supports Democratic candidate Hillary Clinton in the 2016 presidential election. In the final days of the 2020 presidential campaign, she explicitly supports Democratic candidate Joe Biden.

She also supports the LGBT cause with Jay-Z and pays tribute to her uncle Johnny, whom she cites as "the most fabulous gay man I've ever known who helped raise me and my sister", with a speech at the 2019 GLAAD Media Awards.

Charities

From an early age, Beyoncé was aware of social problems. Her father sometimes took her to charities, particularly in African-American society. Beyoncé and Destiny's Child member Kelly Rowland, along with Rowland's family, founded the Survivor Foundation, a charity set up to provide transitional housing for victims of 2005's Hurricane Katrina and storm evacuees in the Houston, Texas area. The Survivor Foundation thus extends the humanitarian mission of the Knowles-Rowland Youth Center, a multi-purpose community outreach center located in downtown Houston. Beyoncé donates $100,000 to the Gulf Coast Ike Relief Fund, for victims of Hurricane Ike in the Houston area. She organizes a fundraiser for Hurricane Ike victims through the Survivor Foundation.

In 2001, she took part with dancer Marie Bellois and some thirty other top stars in *What More Can I Give*, a Michael Jackson song whose proceeds from digital sales went to benefit associations for American children.

In 2005, music producer David Foster, his daughter Amy Foster-Gillies, and Beyoncé wrote *Stand Up for Love*, to serve as the anthem for World Children's Day, an event held worldwide every year on November 20 to raise awareness and funds for children's causes. Destiny's Child lend their voices and support to the cause, serving as global ambassadors for the 2005 World Children's Day program. In 2008, Beyoncé recorded *Just Stand Up!* with various artists, a charity single for the Stand U Cancer charity. Other singers involved include Mariah Carey, Leona Lewis, Rihanna, LeAnn Rimes and Mary J. Blige.

Beyoncé holds food drives during breaks in her The Beyoncé Experience tour in Houston on July 14, Atlanta on July 20, Washington D.C. on August 9, Toronto on August 15, Chicago on August 18, and Los Angeles on September 2, 2006. On October 4, 2008, Beyoncé attended the Miami Children's Hospital Diamond Ball & Private Concert at the American Airlines Arena in Miami, where she was inducted into the International Pediatric Hall of Fame. 7-year-old Ethan Bortnick performs *Over the Rainbow*, which he dedicates to Beyoncé. After the *Cadillac Records* film closes, Beyoncé donates her full fee to Phoenix House, a national organization of drug rehab centers. Beyoncé visits Brooklyn, New York, to prepare for her role as heroin-addicted singer Etta James. On March 5, 2010, Beyoncé and her mother, Tina Knowles, open the Beyoncé Cosmetology Center at the Brooklyn Phoenix House. The program offers seven months of cosmetology training for men and women. L'Oréal donates all the products used at the center, and Beyoncé, accompanied by her mother, pledges to donate $100,000 a year.

More recently, Beyoncé has teamed up with the anti-hunger initiative "Show Your Helping Hand" and the General Mills Hamburger Helper. The goal is to fight hunger in America by donating over 3.5 million meals to local food banks. Beyoncé encourages fans to bring their own non-perishable food items to her U.S. concert dates.

Beyoncé has been chosen to appear on the Council of Fashion Designers of America's limited edition "Fashion For Haiti" T-shirt. The T-shirt, which reads "To Haiti With Love", was designed by Peter Arnell, who also created the "Fashion for America" T-shirt that raised two million dollars after September 11.

In October 2020, Beyoncé released a statement saying she had worked with the Feminist Coalition to help supporters of the End SARS movement in Nigeria, including covering medical costs for injured protesters, covering legal costs for arrested protesters and providing food, emergency shelter, transport and telecommunications to those in need. Beyoncé has also shown her support for those fighting other issues in Africa, such as the Anglophone crisis in Cameroon, ShutItAllDown in Namibia, *Zimbabwean Lives Matter* in Zimbabwe and the National Rape Emergency in Liberia. In December 2020, Beyoncé donated $500,000 to help alleviate the U.S. housing crisis caused by the end of the eviction moratorium, awarding 100 $5,000 grants to individuals and families facing foreclosure and eviction.

Privacy policy

Concerning the Destiny's Child turmoil in 2000, Beyoncé admitted in December 2006 that she had suffered from depression due to an accumulation of struggles. The departure of LeToya Luckett and LaTavia Roberson from the group, media attacks, criticism and blogs led to her collapse, as did the break-up with a long-time boyfriend (whom she had had between the ages of 12 and 19), Lyndall Locke, who later revealed that Beyoncé's growing career had taken its toll on their relationship, as she had driven them apart and he no longer felt up to the task.

The depression was so severe that it lasted for two years. She sometimes stayed in her room for days and refused to eat anything. Beyoncé says she found it hard to talk about her depression because Destiny's Child had just won their first Grammy Award, and she was afraid no one would take her seriously. All these events made her question herself and her friends. She describes her feelings: "Now that I'm famous, I'm afraid I'll never find someone new who likes me for who I am. I was afraid to make new friends." She recalls her mother, Tina Knowles, finally telling her to help her out of her depression: "Why do you think no one can love you? Don't you see how smart and beautiful and sweet you are?"

Since 2001', Beyoncé has been in a relationship with Jay-Z, with whom she will collaborate on several occasions. Rumors of their relationship began to circulate after their duet on '03 Bonnie & Clyde, released in October 2002. Despite persistent rumors, they remained discreet on the subject'. In 2005, rumors spread about the couple's marriage. Beyoncé puts them to rest, claiming that she and Jay-Z are not even engaged. When asked in September 2007, Jay-Z replies, "Someday soon, let's put it that way." Laura Schreffler, editor-in-chief of *OK!* magazine, writes: "These people value their privacy."

On April 4, 2008, Beyoncé and Jay-Z got married in New York. The event was made public on April 22, 2008. Beyoncé did not publicly show her wedding ring until the *Fashion Rocks* concert on September 5, 2008 in New York. She finally reveals their marriage in an opening video montage at the *I Am... Sasha Fierce* listening party at the Sony Club in Manhattan.

A report broadcast on *60 Minutes* in 2010 shows that she was home-schooled as a child and prayed before every performance.

On January 7, 2012, Beyoncé gave birth to her first child, a baby girl named Blue Ivy, in New York. On February 1er 2017, Beyoncé announced that she was expecting twins" with a series of photographs and a poem entitled *I have 3 hearts* playing on religious codes. Her pregnancy announcement on Instagram becomes the site's most liked photo in less than a few hours.

In the documentary Homecoming, Beyoncé reveals that during her second pregnancy, she suffers from toxemia and pre-eclampsia. On June 13, 2017, she gave birth to her twins, a boy, Sir Carter and a girl, Rumi Carter.

Discography

Albums Studios

- 2003: *Dangerously in Love*

- 2006: *B'Day*

- 2008: *I Am... Sasha Fierce*

- 2011 : *4*

- 2013 : *Beyoncé*

- 2016 : *Lemonade*

- 2022: *Renaissance*

Extended Plays

- 2007: *Irreemplazable*

- 2012: *4: The Remix*

- 2014: *More*

Collaborative album

- 2018: *Everything Is Love* (with Jay-Z)

Tours

Top of the bill

- *Dangerously in Love World Tour* (2003)

- *The Beyoncé Experience* (2007)

- *I Am... World Tour* (2009-2010)

- *I Am... Yours* (2009)

- *Live at Roseland: Elements of 4* (2011)

- *The Mrs. Carter Show World Tour* (2013)

- *The Formation World Tour* (2016)

With other

- *Verizon Ladies First Tour* with Alicia Keys and Missy Elliott (2004)

- *On The Run Tour* with Jay-Z (2014)

- *On The Run Tour II* with Jay-Z (2018)

Awards and nominations

Beyoncé Knowles is the most awarded artist in the history of the Grammy Awards, with a total of 32 wins.

She is also the most nominated artist in the history of the Grammy Awards, with 88 nominations.

Filmography

Cinema

- 2001: *Carmen: A Hip Hopera* by Robert Townsend : Carmen

- 2002: *Austin Powers in* Jay Roach's *Goldmember*: Foxxy Cleopatra

- 2004: *The Fighting Temptations* by Jonathan Lynn: Lilly

- 2006: *The Pink Panther* by Shawn Levy: Xania

- 2007: *Dreamgirls* by Bill Condon: Deena Jones

- 2008: *Cadillac Records* by Darnell Martin: Etta James

- 2009: *Obsessed* by Steve Shill: Sharon Charles

- 2009: *Wubb Idol (en)* by Larry Hall, James Burks, Steve Daye, Ron Crown: Shine

- 2013: *Epic: The Battle of the Secret Realm* by Chris Wedge: Queen Tara (original voice)

- 2013: *Mademoiselle C.* by Fabien Constant: Elle-même

- 2013 : *Life Is But a Dream (en)* by Beyoncé, Ed Burke, Ilan Y. Benatar: Beyoncé

- 2019 : *The Lion King* by Jon Favreau: Nala

- 2020 : Beyoncé's *Black is King*: a spiritual guide

French-speaking voices

For the French versions, Beyoncé is dubbed by Maïk Darah (*Austin Powers in Goldmember* and *Cadillac Records*), Ingrid Donnadieu (*Epic: La Bataille du royaume secret* and *Dreamgirls*) and Claire Beaudoin (*The Fighting Temptations*). In Quebec, Hélène Mondoux is the actress' most regular voice (*The Pink Panther*, *Austin Powers*, etc.). For *Epic, it's* Geneviève Désilets.

Short films

- 2014: *Run* by Melina Matsoukas: Herself

Homecoming

Beyonce releases the documentary *Homecoming* on digital platform Netflix on April 17, 2019. The self-directed film features her historic concert at California's Coachella festival in 2018, as well as behind-the-scenes footage.

Other books by United Library

https://campsite.bio/unitedlibrary

Milton Keynes UK
Ingram Content Group UK Ltd.
UKHW020732131123
432471UK00004B/40